W9-BUS-684

March

3 1800 00312 2237

K.C. KELLEY • BOB OSTROM

The Child's World

Published by The Child's World®
1980 Lookout Drive • Mankato, MN 56003-1705
800-599-READ • www.childsworld.com

Acknowledgments
The Child's World®: Mary Berendes, Publishing Director
The Design Lab: Design
Jody Jensen Shaffer: Editing and Fact-Checking

Photo credits
© Aaron Settipane/Dreamstime.com: 23 (bottom); BuddikaS/
Shutterstock.com: 18; catwalker/Shutterstocjk.com: 22 (top);
cynoclub/Shutterstock.com: 12 (bottom); EdrZambrano/iStock.
com: 10; Laurence Agron/Dreamstime.com: 22 (bottom); leaf/
iStock.com: 11 (top); Library of Congress: 19 (top); littleny/
Shutterstock.com: 11(bottom); Lusine/Shutterstock.com: cover,
1, 5; National Aeronautics and Space Administration: 20 (top);
Oren Jack Turner/Wikimedia Commons; 23 (top); PHOTO 999/
Shutterstock.com: 12 (bottom); Shebeko/Shutterstock.com: 13
(top); Splosh/Dreamstime.com: 20 (bottom); Supreme Court of the
United States/Wikimedia Commons: 23 (middle); Tobias Arhelger/
Shutterstock.com: 12 (top); Vinicius Tupinamba/Dreamstime.com:
6; Zainkapasi/Dreamstime.com: 19

Copyright © 2015 by The Child's World®
All rights reserved. No part of this book may be reproduced or
utilized in any form or by any means without written permission
from the publisher.

ISBN 9781626873698
LCCN 2014930708

Printed in the United States of America
Mankato, MN
July, 2014
PA02214

ABOUT THE AUTHOR

K.C. Kelley has written dozens of books for young readers on
everything from sports to nature to history. He was born in
January, loves April because that's when baseball begins, and
loves to take vacations in August!

ABOUT THE ILLUSTRATOR

Bob Ostrom has been illustrating books for twenty years.
A graduate of the New England School of Art & Design at
Suffolk University, Bob has worked for such companies as
Disney, Nickelodeon, and Cartoon Network. He lives in North
Carolina with his wife and three children.

Contents

WELCOME TO MARCH!

Goodbye, winter. Hello, spring! March is the month when winter ends. Spring begins on March 20. Flowers bloom and birds fill the trees. In March, many farmers start planting crops.

MARCH

FACT BOX

Order: Third

Days: 31

HOW DID MARCH GET ITS NAME?

March is named for the Roman god of war, Mars. We get the names of all the months from the ancient Romans. March was actually the first month of the year in their calendar. Names of months came from other gods, from real people, and from numbers.

BAAAA AND ROAR!

"March comes in like a lion and goes out like a lamb."
      —Folk saying
That means the weather in early March is often stormy. The weather in late March is much better!

Birthstone

Each month has a stone linked to it. People who have birthdays in that month call it their birthstone. For March, it's aquamarine.

MARCH AROUND THE WORLD

Here is the name of this month in other languages.

Chinese	sān yuè
Dutch	Maart
English	March
French	Mars
German	der März
Italian	Marzo
Japanese	sangatsu
Spanish	Marzo
Swahili	Machi

WINTER TURNS INTO SPRING

In March, the seasons officially change. Winter becomes spring on the Spring **Equinox** (EE-kwuh-noks). The word means "equal night." On March 20 or 21, the sun is right above the equator. Day and night are the same length. As spring moves on, days become longer and nights shorter.

BIG MARCH HOLIDAYS

St. Patrick's Day, March 17

More than 1,600 years ago, a boy named Patrick was kidnapped from England and taken to Ireland. He was held for six years. During that time, he became a Christian. He escaped from Ireland but later returned to tell the people about what he had learned. Irish people around the world now celebrate his memory on March 17.

HELLO, BIRDS!

Every March 19, people gather near a church in San Juan Capistrano, California. For hundreds of years, they have watched the skies on that day. Each year, the swallows return! The birds swoop into the small town every year. They build their

International Women's Day, March 8

For hundreds of years, women were not allowed to vote or own property. Many people—men and women—began to feel that was not right. In the early 1900s, women began to demand their rights. In 1909, the first Women's Day was held to help that cause. The next year, it spread to other countries and has been held ever since.

MARCH MADNESS!

Basketball fans go crazy during March! American college basketball **tournaments** are played this month. Millions of fans watch games every day. They cheer for their favorite schools and players. The final game is often held in April, but the tournament is known as March Madness!

FUN MARCH DAYS

March has more ways to celebrate than just picking four-leafed clovers on St. Patrick's Day! Here are some of the unusual holidays you can enjoy in March:

MARCH 1

National Peanut Butter Lovers' Day

MARCH 6

National Dentist Day

MARCH 10

International Day of Awesomeness

MARCH 11

Johnny Appleseed Day

MARCH 14

National Potato Chip Day

MARCH 23

National Puppy Day

MARCH WEEKS AND MONTHS

Holidays don't just mean days…you can celebrate for a week, too! You can also have fun all month long. Find out more about these ways to enjoy March!

MARCH WEEKS

National Bubble Week: This holiday was started by a company that makes bubbles. But so what? It's fun to blow bubbles any week of the year!

National Cheerleading Week: In the first full week of March, celebrate students who help others get excited! Thousands of young people take part in cheerleading for their schools.

American Chocolate Week: Looking for a good deal on this sweet stuff? In the third week of March, many candy stores have special deals on chocolate!

MARCH MONTHS

National Red Cross Month: The Red Cross was founded in 1881 by American nurse Clara Barton. The group started out helping wounded soldiers. Today, it helps in disasters around the world.

Women's History Month: Along with International Women's Day, celebrate the great things women have done in history. (Or should we say, "her-story?")

Music in Our Schools Month: For many people, music is a big part of their lives. Schools are a great way to learn music. Concerts and events this month encourage students to study music.

National Umbrella Month: Well, it does rain a lot in March!

MARCH AROUND THE WORLD

Countries around the world celebrate in March. Find these countries on the map. Then read about how people there have fun in March!

MARCH 9

Baron Bliss Day, Belize
A sailor from Portugal visited this Central American country in 1926. He fell in love with it and when he died, he left the country a lot of money. This day says, "Thanks, Baron!"

A COLORFUL FESTIVAL

During the days around the full moon each March, Hindu people in India and elsewhere celebrate *Holi*. Known as the Festival of Colors, it welcomes spring. People fling colored powder all over themselves and others!

MARCH 11

Day of Restoration of Independence, Lithuania

On this day in 1990, Lithuania became the first country to break away from the Soviet Union.

MARCH 25

Greek National Day, Cyprus

This island in the Mediterranean Sea split from Great Britain officially on this day in 1960.

MARCH 12

Youth Day, Zambia

This African country is one of many to celebrate this day honoring its young people with festivals and concerts.

MARCH IN HISTORY

March 1, 1872

Yellowstone becomes the first **national park** in the world. Today, the U.S. has more than 400 National Parks and other protected areas. Hundreds more are located around the world.

IDES OF MARCH

Julius Caesar was a leader in ancient Rome. Some did not want him to be leader. In 44 BCE, on March 15 (known as the "Ides" or "middle" of March), Caesar was killed. Today, people still say, "Beware the Ides of March."

March 2, 1962

Wilt Chamberlain of the Philadelphia 76ers scored 100 points in an NBA game. That's still the most ever scored by one player!

March 10, 1876

Alexander Graham Bell made the first telephone call. He called to his assistant, "Mr. Watson, come here. I want to see you."

March 11, 1931

Work on the Hoover Dam began. Later standing more than 726 feet tall, the dam helps Western states have electricity.

March 12, 1912

Juliette Low founded the Girl Scouts.

March 18, 1965

Soviet cosmonaut Alexei Leonov became the first person to walk in space.

March 20, 1999

Brian Jones and Bertrand Piccard landed their huge balloon. They had just finished the first round-the-world balloon flight!

March 31, 1889

The Eiffel Tower opened to the public in Paris, France.

NEW STATES!

Five states first joined the United States in March. Do you live in any of these? If you do, then make sure and say, "Happy Birthday!" to your state.

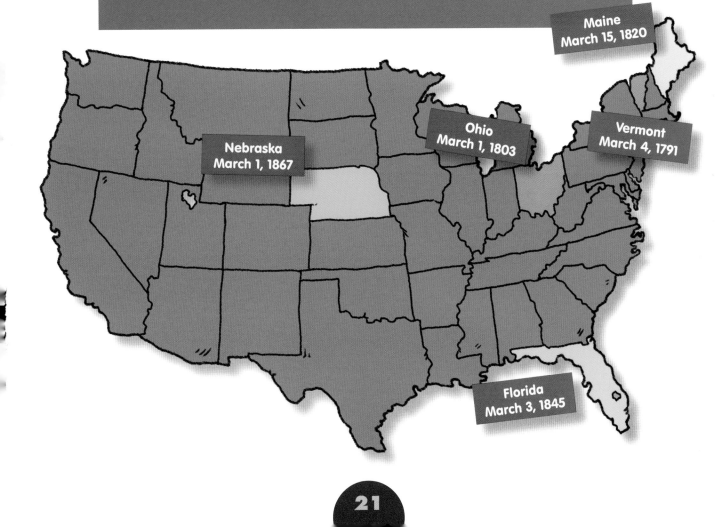

Maine
March 15, 1820

Ohio
March 1, 1803

Vermont
March 4, 1791

Nebraska
March 1, 1867

Florida
March 3, 1845

FAMOUS MARCH BIRTHDAYS

March 2

Dr. Seuss
In March, this writer was born.
To celebrate, go toot a horn!

March 3

Alexander Graham Bell
This scientist and inventor
invented the telephone.

March 6

Shaquille O'Neal
The only thing bigger than this NBA
great was his list of nicknames: Shaq
Daddy, Shaq Fu, The Big Aristotle,
Diesel, the Real Deal...and more!

March 14

Albert Einstein

This German scientist created a new way to think about space and time.

March 15

Ruth Bader Ginsburg

She joined the U.S. Supreme Court in 1993.

March 24

Peyton Manning

Manning was already an NFL superstar before he came back from a neck injury to join the Denver Broncos in 2012.

March 27

Mariah Carey

This superstar singer and entertainer hit it big in 1990 with her first album. She's been very popular ever since.

GLOSSARY

Christian (KRISS-chun) A person who believes in the teachings of a man named Jesus of Nazareth.

equinox (EE-kwuh-noks) One of two times a year when the daytime and nighttime are the same length.

national park (NASH-un-ull PARK) A section of land set aside by the government for people to enjoy.

tournaments (TURN-uh-ments) Contests in which people or teams try to win a championship.

INDEX

APR 16 2015

CENTRAL ISLIP PUBLIC LIBRARY

3 1800 00312 2237

312 2237

J508.
2
KEL

Kelley, K.C.

March

$25.64

Central Islip Public Library
33 Hawthrone Avenue
Central Islip, NY 11722